Volume One
For Children Ages 3-6

Developed & Written by
SUSAN AMERIKANER

Illustrated by
TONY GLEASON

Creative Consultant:
Sarina Simon

A TOM DOHERTY ASSOCIATES BOOK

To Jeannette Glass, my mother, who taught me
that when one door closes, another one always opens—
if you push it hard enough.

101 THINGS TO DO TO DEVELOP YOUR CHILD'S GIFTS & TALENTS:
VOLUME ONE FOR CHILDREN AGES 3–6

A TOR Book
Published by Tom Doherty Associates, Inc.
49 West 24 Street
New York, NY 10010

Cover art by Doug Fornuff
Book design by Stacey Simons/Neuwirth & Associates

ISBN: 0-812-59497-5   Can. ISBN: 0-812-59498-3

Library of Congress Catalog Card Number: 88-51641

First edition: May 1989

Printed in the United States of America

0 9 8 7 6 5 4 3 2

About the Author

Susan Amerikaner specializes in making education fun for children and adults. A native of Baltimore, Maryland, she received her bachelor's degree in creative writing from the University of Maryland and her Master of Arts in Teaching from George Washington University.

As a teacher in Montgomery County, Maryland, Amerikaner taught every elementary grade level and served as school coordinator of activities for gifted and talented students. Mickey Mouse interrupted her teaching career and transplanted Amerikaner to Los Angeles, where she developed a line of classroom materials for the Walt Disney Educational Media Company.

Amerikaner has written several children's books, including *It's O.K. to Say No to Drugs!* She is the creator and author of the *Gifted and Talented Workbook* series.

Currently a writer and consultant for a number of publishers and media companies, Amerikaner resides in Chatsworth, California, with her husband and two sons.

From the Author

Every parent would like to have a gifted child. Many do, but don't know it! Child-development experts assert that almost every child has some innate gifts and talents which will flourish—if they are nurtured. This book is designed to help you cultivate your child's natural abilities. These activities are appropriate for children from ages three through six, but you are the best judge of whether a particular activity suits your child's level of ability and interest.

While designing a curriculum for gifted elementary-school students, I realized that such a curriculum had a much broader application. Gifted education focuses on teaching children *how to think*. What student doesn't need to learn how to think?

I began using the gifted curriculum in all of my classes, and the results were what I expected. Just about every child improved in the areas of critical and creative thinking.

WHY ARE THINKING SKILLS IMPORTANT?

Critical and creative thinking skills are the skills of logic, reasoning, and imagination which enable a child to learn virtually anything. Facts change. Thinking skills do not. A child who knows how to think and reason effectively will be able to approach new tasks with confidence. A child who knows how to think may not know all the answers, but he or she will know how to find them.

Here are some of the key critical and creative thinking skills emphasized in this book:

Sequencing: putting things in order.

Inference: gathering bits and pieces of information and drawing a conclusion.

Deduction: drawing conclusions by using inference and complex clues, including negative clues.

Creativity: creating original ideas; accumulating details; understanding relationships among things that seem dissimilar; applying imagination when solving problems.

HOW YOU CAN HELP

You don't have to be a teacher or a scientist to encourage your child to think. You simply need to be willing to listen and guide, not unlike a travel agent!

Listening is vital. Listen for questions. Teachers often report that the brightest students ask a lot of questions, and questions open the door to discovery. Sometimes adults unwittingly shut this door by responding too quickly and *giving* answers. When your child asks you a question, encourage him or her to find the answer independently. Be prepared to encounter a certain amount of mess—self-discovery is a messy business. A child looking for answers may spill, break, tear, or bend things.

When you encourage self-discovery, you may find that you have to admit that you don't always know the answers. Then you can join in the experiment or tag along to the library! A good rule of thumb is: try to answer a question with a question. "How do you think we can find out?" is a valuable response.

HOW TO USE THIS BOOK

Each activity in this book is preceded by a brief introduction that states the overall purpose of the activity and outlines the general skills it is designed to reinforce. These are broad guidelines—feel free to stretch an activity and include any other goals or skills you desire.

Sometimes I describe variations of an activity. It's not necessary to try all the variations right away. If you wait, later it will seem like an entirely new activity!

Let your child be your guide. If he or she is bored or tired and doesn't want to finish an activity—don't. Be alert. If your child isn't interested, stop. The directions are labeled "What You *and* Your Child Do" because I hope that you will participate with your child in most of the activities. We are encouraging independent thinking, but the fun can be shared! Also, only you will know how much help your child will need for each activity.

The activities have been designed for their simplicity as well as effectiveness. For most you won't need to buy anything special; you probably will have everything you need around the house.

A SYMBOL TO LOOK FOR

I know how it feels to spend an hour getting an activity ready—only to find that the activity is over in five minutes. Keeping this in mind, I have tried to create activities that require as little preparation as possible. But good preparation is important, and young children enjoy working with their hands. Therefore, when an activity calls for extra setup, I have designated it with this symbol:

ABOUT RIGHT ANSWERS

When I teach thinking skills, I am not worried about getting the *right* answers. I'm trying to motivate children to *look for* answers. I try to teach a child to question, to learn by trial and error and self-discovery. I aim to give a child opportunities, not lessons. This book provides you and your child with 101 such opportunities. I hope you try them all!

Susan Amerikaner

1 A Trick Question

WHAT
YOU
AND
YOUR
CHILD
DO

This is the best "gifted" trick I know, and you can use it every day, starting today. It makes a child turn inward and think about what he or she already feels and knows.

When your child asks you a question, simply say, "What do *you* think?" This works beautifully, even with the youngest child. Like a computer, your child will begin to add up what he or she already knows and try to come up with a solution.

There is an extra benefit for you. You will start to learn *how* your child thinks. You may be surprised. This magical question often prompts responses that you will long remember.

2 | House Secrets

This activity stimulates questions that provoke further research. While you are all having a good time, you are also cultivating skills of observation, inference, and prediction.

WHAT YOU NEED

Flashlight
Hand-held mirror

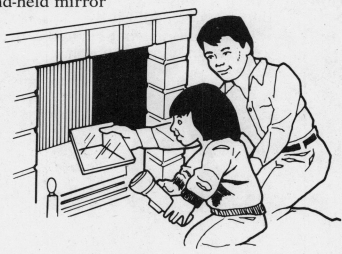

WHAT YOU AND YOUR CHILD DO

Go on a "secret" tour of your home. If you have a basement in your house or apartment building, be sure to include it in this trek. Look at the water pipes, the electric meter, the circuit breaker, or fuse box. Take off the top of the toilet tank and look inside. Find all the heating ducts. Figure out the route that your water takes to get to a bathtub. Your child will think of many more secret places to uncover.

Use the flashlight to look in dark corners. Encourage your child to find ways to use the mirror. For instance, you can use it to look up a chimney. Or you can hide around the corner from someone and watch what he or she is doing!

3 Pictures: Perfect for Language Development

Most of us treasure our photo albums and keep them far from tiny hands. Who wants peanut butter and jelly all over our last glimpse of Aunt Clara? But few things are more engrossing to a child, even a toddler, than family photos. They can be powerful tools for strengthening spoken-language and reading skills.

A spiral notebook with lined paper (You can use a commercial photo album, as long as it has some room for writing under or next to each picture.)

Marker

Snapshots

Tape

Save your photo "seconds." These are the ones that are too light or dark, too far away, too off-center, or for some reason not quite good enough to make the family album. Tape these photos into the notebook. If possible, let your child select and tape the pictures.

Ask your child for a word, phrase, or sentence that describes the picture. Clearly print this beneath the photo. Include the date, too!

This photo album belongs to your child, for him or her to read and look at at any time. Since you've used "seconds," you don't need to worry about sticky fingers. These albums can become a child's first, and most beloved, books, and should periodically be updated.

This activity can also open the door to creative writing and photography. Older children will enjoy taking the pictures themselves. One of my former students began with family albums and then started posing friends and family, creating scenes for his original stories.

4 Match My Coupons!

This is a great way to spend time while you're waiting in line at the supermarket. Not only will this activity make the time pass more quickly; it will enhance your child's visual discrimination ability.

WHAT YOU NEED

Supermarket coupons
Items which you intend
to purchase that
match the coupons

WHAT YOU AND YOUR CHILD DO

Take out the coupons that match items you are buying. Have your child take a coupon and find the corresponding item in your shopping cart.

5 Alphabet Search

Here's an easy way to make travel time go faster and help with reading, language, and observation skills.

WHAT YOU AND YOUR CHILD DO

Point to the first letter **A** you see. Call it out with a complete and descriptive sentence: "I see the letter **A** on the sign over the grocery store!"

Now it's your child's turn to find letter **B** and do the same thing. Keep taking turns and go through the whole alphabet. If finding one letter takes too long and becomes too frustrating, move on to another.

Learning to form complete sentences that give precise information is important. Resist the urge to correct your child when his or her answers are incomplete; just make sure that you use complete sentences. Your child will begin to model his or her responses after yours!

6 | The World's Best Thinking Game

The old standard game of Twenty Questions is just about the best tool there is for developing critical thinking skills, particularly deductive reasoning.

Think of an object and say, "I'm thinking of something in this room." Your child has twenty chances to guess the item by asking questions that can be answered with a simple "yes" or "no."

Younger children inevitably begin by naming things: "Is it the lamp?" "Is it the chair?" When it's your turn, set an example by asking questions that classify and define, such as: "Is it alive?" "Is it bigger than the couch?" "Is it something you wear?"

7

Clock Cards

Most children by the age of four or five can learn to tell time on the hour on a clock face. Half-hours are harder to learn. This is a technique I successfully used to teach time in the classroom and at home. Children seem to catch on to half-hours faster when they can connect the times to personal experiences.

Index cards
Pencil
Markers
Compass or a lid for tracing circles
Old magazines
Glue

Draw or cut out pictures that show typical daily activities. Use activities that occur at the same time each day, such as brushing teeth, eating breakfast, going to school, taking a bath, reading a bedtime story, etc. Glue the pictures to index cards.

On the remaining cards, draw a clock face with the hands indicating the correct time of each activity. It's a good idea to start with the hour only; later you can refine the clock cards. Write A.M. and P.M. on the bottom of the clock faces and review the cards with your child. Match the clock faces with the correct activity.

8 Moonlight Madness

A walk around the block in the dark can be like a visit to a different world. It can also be an opportunity to promote keen observation and descriptive language skills.

Two good flashlights
Appropriate clothing

Before you begin, you should each name three things that you anticipate seeing during your walk. As you walk, point out these things when you see them. Do you see things that look different at night or things that you never noticed in the daylight?

When you are in a safe, not scary, place, turn off the flashlights for a few moments. Be silent. Then describe what you see and hear.

9 Egg Drop

If you're not queasy about messes, this activity gives everyone in your family a workout in problem-solving. There's a solution in the back of the book, but don't peek! You may even discover a new answer.

Lots of raw eggs
Sponges and paper towels
Bucket

Plastic wrap
Water
Newspapers

Your task is to figure out how to drop a raw egg from a height without breaking the egg. You can use all the materials listed. Here's a thought to get you started: you need to find a way to cushion the fall.

Do this in a place that's easy to clean up, such as over a kitchen floor, or outside, near a garden hose. If you do it indoors, make sure you put newspapers on the floor first.

10 Right or Left?

This is another "old faithful" game to sharpen thinking skills. Players must concentrate, remember, and predict.

A coin

Behind your back hide the coin in one of your hands. Your child chooses the hand in which he or she thinks the coin is hiding.

Establish a pattern and ask your child to figure out the pattern (i.e. hide the coin in your right hand, then your left, then right; or hide the coin in your right hand twice, then in your left hand twice).

Noticing a pattern can be difficult, but you can teach your child to look for one. Slowly demonstrate a very simple pattern, pointing out the repetition. Repeat the pattern, but stop in the middle. Can your child predict the next action?

11 Peanut Butter Letters

Learning to write can be frustrating and tedious. Educators recommend that students practice writing with a variety of materials. Forming letters out of clay, sticks, blocks, or other substances helps children remember their shapes. Here is a recipe for scrumptious letter practice.

Please note that this activity takes two days to complete. You can use any amount of peanut butter, honey, and powdered milk, providing you use the correct proportions.

WHAT YOU NEED

One teaspoon of oil
Two parts peanut butter
One part honey
Three parts instant powdered milk
Waxed paper
Medium-size bowl

WHAT YOU AND YOUR CHILD DO

Grease the bowl to keep the ingredients from sticking. Mix the peanut butter and honey. Add the powdered milk a little at a time until the mixture is somewhat stiff. Knead the mixture. Children love to help with this part.

Refrigerate it overnight. Spread out waxed paper. Now you can shape edible letters out of the dough. Make them as thick or as thin as you like!

12 Imagination Station

Never underestimate the power of pretending! It provides practice in language, sequencing, and creative problem-solving skills.

Act out any of the following scenarios:

Walk barefoot on sand
Walk barefoot on wet rocks crossing a stream
Walk in snow; on ice; in water; in mud
Walk like Grandma, or someone else you know
Walk as if you are late, or scared, or tired
Eat something sweet
Eat something sticky
Eat very hot pizza
Eat a melting ice-cream cone

Add your own ideas to this list.

13 Catalog Categories

"Which two are the same?" "What's different?" "Which one does not belong?"

These are all questions that require a child to sort and classify. These skills are usually considered reading readiness skills, but they are much more. They are basic thinking skills and become increasingly complex and useful over time. Classification is a basic tool for scientific inquiry. The zoologist who sorts species of animals probably loved sorting socks and beads as a toddler!

Two or three empty shoe boxes or containers of similar size

Old magazines, catalogs, newspapers, etc.

Scissors

Cut out pictures of things that fit into two different categories. Put each picture into the correct box.

You don't have to cut out all the pictures. After you find the first one, your child can cut out the rest. You can add a third box and another category. In later sessions, your child can select the categories.

Categories You Can Use

Things to sit on

Things to eat

Healthy foods

Junk foods

Happy people

Sad people

Tall people

Short people

Babies

Children

Adults

Food that comes from plants

Food that comes from animals

14 Literary Plus

Here's an easy tip that will give your child a subtle but deeper awareness of literature and art. It is never too early to instill an appreciation of the human creativity behind any product.

A book

Any time you read to your child, make it a habit to tell him or her the name of the book's author and illustrator as well as its title. Repeat this information at the end of the book, and if there is biographical information, read this aloud, too.

Encourage your child to remember authors and illustrators and their work. "Oh, Maurice Sendak! We read one of his books before. Do you remember it? What do you think this one will be about?" At the end of the book you could ask how this story compared to other books you've read together.

15 Shiny Pennies

This is a chemistry experiment guaranteed to dazzle your child.

Four tablespoons of salt	Paper towels
½ cup vinegar	Empty cup or jar
Old pennies	Spoon

Pour the vinegar into a cup or jar. Add salt and stir until it has dissolved. Now drop in the pennies. The coins will look better in a few minutes, but if you leave them in the solution overnight, the results are really terrific. Remove the pennies with the spoon and drain them on paper towels.

A friend of mine tried this with her son and then realized that she had finally found the perfect (and economical) polish for her copper pans!

16 Having a Heat Wave

Children are fascinated by thermometers. They don't need to know about Fahrenheit or Centigrade to understand that a thermometer measures heat. Here are some simple suggestions to help get this concept across.

An inexpensive indoor/outdoor thermometer
Paper
Pencil

Show your child how to read the thermometer. Don't worry about degrees. Just explain that the higher the reading, the warmer the temperature.

Make a list of different places (inside and outside) to check with the thermometer. Take readings at these locations and record the results.

Ask questions: Why do you think it was colder in the living room than the laundry room? What will happen if we take the temperature again at night? Where is the warmest part of your room?

17 Making Rainbows

This simple demonstration of rainbows turns superstition into science. It should also provoke more questions about light and color. Let your child's questions carry you to the library, where you can find real gold.

Garden hose
Small mirror
Glass of water

Explain that sunlight is made up of many colors (red, orange, yellow, green, blue, indigo [a deep blue], and violet). Raindrops bend light and divide it into these different colors.

Here are two ways to demonstrate this natural wonder:

Turn your back to the sun and spray a thin spray of water from the hose. (You may need to try holding a finger over the nozzle.) A rainbow should be visible.

Place a mirror in a glass of water. Place the glass in a spot where the sun hits it. Turn the glass around until you see a rainbow on the wall or ceiling.

Think of other times you have seen rainbows. Was there water to bend the light? Where did the water come from?

18 Sequence Sharpener

Putting things in the correct order is another basic thinking skill that starts out easy but can become more and more challenging.

Old magazines or newspapers
Scissors
Paste or glue
Construction paper or any plain, unlined paper
Crayons or markers

WHAT YOU AND YOUR CHILD DO

Find pictures that lend themselves to the question, "What happens next?" For example, a picture of a child with a dirty face.

Draw two boxes on the unlined paper. Number the boxes. Paste a picture in Box One. Ask your child to imagine what will happen next and draw this prediction in Box Two.

Here are two variations:

> Paste a picture in the second box and ask your child to fill in the first with a picture that shows what happened before.

> Draw and label three boxes. Put a picture in the middle and ask your child to draw what happened before and after.

15

19 Taste Buds

One of my colleagues pointed out that many of my best educational ideas are food-related. It's true. I love food and haven't found many kids who don't.

This activity calls for tasting and classifying.

Please be sure to let your child know that it is *not acceptable* to experiment with food without your supervision.

WHAT YOU NEED

Assorted foods: salty, sweet, and sour

WHAT YOU AND YOUR CHILD DO

Explain that each food belongs to one of three groups. Have your child taste each item and divide the collection into three groups. Ask your child to name each group. How did he or she know which food belonged to which group?

20 Mystery Sock

One very long, very rainy day in my kindergarten class I invented this game. It became an instant hit. It's a fine way to reinforce problem-solving and reading readiness skills.

WHAT YOU NEED

A clean sock
Plastic letters

Where your child cannot see, place one letter in the sock. Tie off the top of the sock. Have your child feel the sock and guess what letter is inside.

Start by using uppercase letters. Lowercase letters are a real challenge. For older children, put in three letters that spell out a simple word (for example: cat, hat, top, sit). Have your child identify the letters, and then unscramble them to spell the word.

21 Magnet Magic

Magnets are great science lures for young children. Few can resist the delight of trying to see which objects attract and which do not. This simple trial and error method is the foundation of scientific inquiry. Use a magnet to pull your child into science!

A magnet
Two paper bags (small shopping
bags with handles would be perfect)
Marker

Label one bag "YES" and the other "NO." Go through the house and around the yard with your child and find things that stick to the magnet. Put the items in the correct bag: "YES" if they stick; "NO" if they don't. If the objects are too big for the bags, mark them with masking tape and a marker or with "stick-on" paper notes.

When you're all done, ask: "What seems to be the same about the things that stick to the magnet?" Can your child use the magnet to find out which objects contain metal and which do not?

Sounds Like . . .

Have you ever heard an educator talk about "auditory discrimination"? To identify sounds a person must think and listen at the same time. That's not as easy as it sounds!

A selection of five or six household items that make distinct sounds (for example: zipper, crunchy food, lamp, typewriter, soda can with "pop" top, keys)

Arrange the items on a table. You can show them to your child, but this is more challenging if he or she does not see the items first. Have your child turn away and close his or her eyes.

Ask your child to identify the sounds you make, one at a time. Chew the carrot, zip and unzip the zipper, type, jiggle the keys, etc.

This is one of those instant games that is fun for everyone in the family. Take turns gathering items and making sounds.

It's a Toss-up

This is a classroom game that makes a fine transition to the home. My children love it, and I love the painless way it reinforces basic math facts.

Marker
Lid of a shirt or gift box
Three Ping-Pong balls
Ten paper cups
Glue

Write numerals from one to ten on the bottom of each cup. Glue cups to the box lid. Each player tosses three balls into the cups and then adds up the score. To practice with sums up to twenty or beyond, add more cups and more balls.

Raisins in the Sun

This is a classic early-childhood science lesson that demonstrates evaporation. Make sure your child doesn't miss it. It takes a few sunny days to complete this demonstration.

Seedless grapes
Paper plate
Piece of cheesecloth

Remove grapes from the stems and wash and dry them. Place the grapes on the plate and cover them with the cheesecloth. Put the plate in direct sunlight and leave them there for four to five days, turning them over occasionally.

After several days, squeeze the grapes to see if they are dried out. If there is still moisture in the fruit, leave them in the sun. When the grapes are all dry, you have homemade raisins. Eat and enjoy!

Ask your child how he or she thinks the grapes changed into raisins. Where did the "juice" go? Does this happen to any other foods?

25 Time Plates

In the classroom I found that many students could not tell time by reading the hands of a clock because their homes were full of digital clocks! Here is a delicious way to practice telling time, along with sequencing and inference skills.

Bite-size foods such as raisins or grapes
One large, flat, round plate

Place the empty plate on a table. Imagine that it is the face of a clock. Where would three o'clock be? Six o'clock? Two o'clock? Point to the correct locations.

Arrange the food items on the clock face. Put one raisin on one o'clock, one at two o'clock, and so on. Now give directions:

"Eat the raisin that shows the hour just before three o'clock."

"Eat the raisin that shows the time you go to bed."

"Eat the raisin that shows the hour two hours after you get home from school."

26 | Perfect Fit

This super-easy activity nurtures the ability to make comparisons and predictions. It's especially appropriate for very young children. It seems so simple, but there is a lot of math readiness packed into it.

Twelve empty jars and lids of different sizes and shapes

Line up the jars on the table. Take off the lids and mix them up. Have your child match each lid to the correct jar.

27 Sweet Letters To Trace

One of my fellow teachers told me about this technique for helping children trace letters. Educators affirm that it is helpful to teach a child a skill in more than one mode. In this case your child is using the sense of touch as well as sight.

WHAT YOU NEED

Dry flavored gelatin or pudding mix. Use the kind with real sugar. The others will taste bitter.

Waxed paper

WHAT YOU AND YOUR CHILD DO

Spread a thin, even layer of the dry mix on the waxed paper. Your child can trace letters in the mix with his or her fingers. Finger licking is allowed!

Sink or Float?

This is a simple activity that introduces the concepts of weight, texture, structure, and composition. It also forces a child to observe, predict, classify, and draw conclusions.

WHAT YOU NEED

Plastic trash can, large bucket, or sink with a good stopper
One small plastic bottle or container, without lid
Assortment of household items

WHAT YOU AND YOUR CHILD DO

Fill the bucket with lukewarm water. Gather an assortment of items. Holding each item, ask: "Do you think this will sink or float?" Record the guesses. Now test them!

As you test each item, you should discover that, in general, heavy things sink and lighter ones float. The plastic container can be used to demonstrate that hollow things float until they fill up with water.

29 | Tick? Tick?

Here's a "quickie" that will help your child's listening and concentration skills.

A loud kitchen timer

Hide the timer and have your child find it!
Although it is unrealistic to expect a child under five to learn to read a clock, this game presents an excellent opportunity for a brief introduction. Use the timer itself to show how long it took to find it. Challenge your child to find it sooner on the next try.

30 | Find the Mistake

Your child will love listening for your mistakes! In the meantime, you will be sharpening listening skills and thinking skills, such as classification and inference.

Explain that you are going to recite a list of words that begin with the same sound, and that you will make one mistake. One word will not belong.
Tell your child to clap when you make the mistake. Here's a sample list: go, get, girl, gorilla, sit, gate, gooey, fooey, grass, good.
This game is wonderful because it is so simple yet

so versatile. The sample word list stresses recognizing the beginnings of words, but other kinds of things can be substituted. Here are some possible categories:

animals

plants

words that end with the same sounds

fruits

things that fly

things that
have wheels

small things

big things

red things or blue, or yellow, etc.

words that rhyme

words that describe a particular animal, item, or location

31 Air Today

This demonstration never fails to amaze. I once began a school year with this "magic trick." By the end of the year my kindergarten class had learned enough scientific magic to give the whole school a magic show. After all, a magician is just a scientist in a top hat.

WHAT YOU NEED

One glass

One piece of newspaper or other paper

Sink or bucket partially filled with water

Crumple up the piece of paper and put it in the bottom of the glass. Turn the glass upside down. Before doing anything more, ask your child what he or she thinks will happen to the paper when you put the glass into the water. After he or she has answered, hold the glass absolutely straight and plunge it into the water.

Hold the glass in this position for a few seconds. Remove it and take out the paper. Is the paper wet or dry? What kept the water from reaching the paper? (Air)

Try this experiment again. What happens if the glass is not held straight? Why?

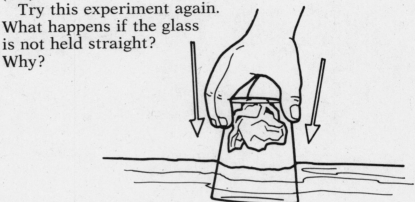

32 Blocks Plus

Get out those dusty building blocks and cultivate creative thinking skills through dramatic play!

Building blocks
Paper
Markers
Tape
Ice-cream sticks or toothpicks (optional)
Clay or modeling dough (optional)

When your child shows you a new block structure, make signs to label it (for example: Nina's Castle or Witches' Kitchen). If your child is learning to write, encourage him or her to make the signs. Help with spelling, of course!

You can tape the signs directly onto the blocks, or tape them to ice-cream sticks or toothpicks and stand them in lumps of clay.

33 Attribute Game

Attributes are those qualities or characteristics which distinguish objects or people. Attributes are easier to find than to describe. The following game is an easy one, similar to "Twenty Questions."

Old magazines, catalogs, newspapers
Scissors

27

Cut out pictures of objects, people, animals, and plants from the magazines. Spread ten pictures out on a table. Mentally select one picture.

Describe the picture to your child by listing its attributes, one at a time. Try to make your description progress from general to specific. For example:

See how far you get before your child can identify the picture. Take turns guessing and giving clues.

• "IT IS ALIVE"
    • "IT GROWS"
        • "IT IS A PLANT"
            • "IT HAS LEAVES"

34 | Rainbow Rhymes

Rhyming is irresistible to most children, and it is a brilliant tool for encouraging creative thinking. This activity also stretches oral and written vocabulary.

Crayons or markers
Paper

Take turns rhyming a word and a color, such as "blue shoe," "pink ink," "red head." Get as silly as you like! Draw pictures of the items and label them.

"BLUE"....

...."SHOE"

35 Contract and Expand

Take advantage of a child's interest in balloons. Use this family activity to demonstrate the concept that heat usually causes "things to get bigger" (heat makes molecules expand), and cold makes them "smaller" (cold makes molecules contract).

Two mixing bowls
Two balloons
One soda bottle
Water

Fit a deflated balloon over the neck of the bottle. Fill one mixing bowl with ice water. Fill the other with very hot water. Place the bottle into the bowl of hot water. The balloon should slowly fill up with air.

Once the balloon has inflated, place the bottle into the bowl of ice water. What happens?

Relate this experiment to other events. What happens when we put a cake in the oven? What happens when ice cream melts?

36 Spinning Tales

The ability to relate seemingly unrelated things in unique ways is one of the hallmarks of a creative thinker. The next activity will give your child a good start in that direction.

Index cards
Scissors
Glue or tape
Old magazines, newspapers, etc.

Cut out lots of pictures that fit into each of the following categories: people, animals, food, and objects. Paste the pictures on the index cards.

Gather together all the people cards. Shuffle them and place them face down. Put all of the other cards together. Shuffle them and place them in a second pile, also face down.

Have your child pick two cards from the people pile and four from the other pile. Place the cards face up. Ask your child to tell a story using all six cards. Let him or her think for three or four minutes, rearranging the cards if he or she wishes.

Take turns with your child. It may not be easy to relate a hot dog, a hammer, a blue bird, a baby, a telephone, and someone's grandfather—but you may be surprised at the results!

37 | Read All About It

Your refrigerator is a splendid place to display all the family news that's fit to print. Creating a newspaper is one of the best ways to stimulate creative writing and practice basic language skills.

WHAT YOU NEED

Paper
Markers or crayons
Pencils
Magnets or tape
Refrigerator

WHAT YOU AND YOUR CHILD DO

Think about one special thing that happened during the week. Did your child get new clothes, learn a new song, go to the dentist, or make a new friend? Use markers to write a simple headline:

For a real newspaper look, add a picture and print a simple caption beneath. Make a new page each week. At the end of the month, put the pages together. Be sure to date them—this monthly gazette may become a family keepsake.

In our house this has become a family venture, with Mom and Dad adding their own news. Sometimes we make copies and sent them to Grandma.

Find the Worm

This really isn't about worms. It is a game that enhances concentration and shape discrimination, but the title is irresistible to most young children!

Five or more different shapes of pasta
Scarf or some type of blindfold
Bowl

Place a handful of each pasta shape into the bowl. Mix them up. Look carefully at each different shape. Then cover your child's eyes with the blindfold.

Give your child one piece of pasta. He or she must put the other hand into the bowl and find three pieces that are the same shape.

You can do this with raw pasta first; then try it cooked. Be sure to run cold water on the cooked pasta so it doesn't stick together. Now it's *really* like finding worms!

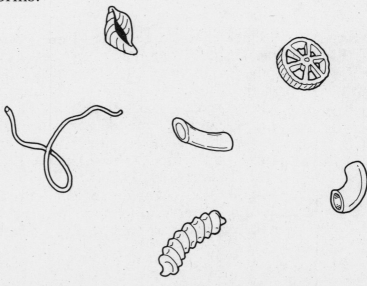

Magic Changes

Encouraging a child to be "more creative" sounds mystical. It isn't. As with most educational objectives, it is best achieved by providing specific tasks. This simple game is designed to help a child generate many creative connections.

Think of a new way to use a familiar object. Could you imagine using a table as a sled? How about using a rake to scratch a giant's back? Remember, one of the nice things about creativity is that it includes being silly.

Take turns with your child and "change" ordinary household items into something new. Here are some objects to start with: toothbrush, shoe, broom, cookie pan, spoon, bed, sofa, chair, and lamp.

Drawing pictures of these new inventions may be too difficult for some children. But since some of these ideas would be wonderful to see, you might keep crayons and paper handy!

Aquabet Blocks

Here is a unique way to make your child literally "soak up" reading skills. It is a good example of teaching skills using touch as well as sight.

WHAT YOU NEED

Twenty Styrofoam plates (the trays from meat also work)
Scissors
Pencil or marker
Ruler
Sink or bathtub

WHAT YOU AND YOUR CHILD DO

Draw 3" × 3" squares on the Styrofoam. Draw a block letter inside each square. Uppercase letters are best here. It's also a good idea to make extra **A**'s, **B**'s, **O**'s, and other frequently used letters. Cut out the letters.

Your child will enjoy spelling his or her name and other words in a sink full of water or while bathing. Try the same thing with numbers.

Yes, You Can Read!

Does your preschooler recognize the names of local grocery stores, restaurants, or cereals that he or she sees advertised on TV? This is sight reading, and it is important to point out that this *is* reading! The next time your child blurts out the name of a favorite fast-food place shout with glee: "You can *read!*"

WHAT YOU NEED

Scissors
Newspapers, magazines, etc.
Tape or glue
Markers or crayons
Empty cereal boxes
Poster board

WHAT YOU AND YOUR CHILD DO

Make an "I Can Read" poster. Cut out store names, cereal names, product logos, and any other words that your child can read by sight. Paste the words to the poster.

One family I know started this project on poster board, but ended up buying rolls of white paper and literally papering their child's room!

Scientific Lemonade

You've often heard that simple is best. My own children were amazed by the following demonstration, which is about as simple as you can get.

It encourages a child to observe, predict, analyze results, and apply learning to other situations.

Please note, however, that you must wait a couple of hours for results.

WHAT YOU NEED

Two or three lemons
Two-quart pitcher
Water
Knife

WHAT YOU AND YOUR CHILD DO

Slice each lemon into eight wedges. Put the lemons into the pitcher. Fill the pitcher with water. Place the pitcher in the refrigerator and wait for two or three hours. Taste the water! What has happened? How has the lemon flavor gotten into the water? Explain that the water has helped to break the lemon juice into millions of tiny particles that spread throughout the pitcher. You can't see the particles, but you can taste them in the water. This breaking-down and spreading-out process is called *diffusion*.

Here are some questions for further exploration: When you eat food, does it get broken down and spread out? How? Why is it important for the food to break down inside your body?

43 Mystery Picture

There are many ways to get the most out of a picture book. This activity enhances your child's skills of recall, inference, and deduction.

WHAT YOU NEED

A picture book with twenty-four pages or less

WHAT YOU AND YOUR CHILD DO

Hold the book so that your child can't see it. Turn to a page and describe the picture that you see. Make your description very complete. Close the book, hand it to your child, and ask him or her to find the picture you described.

Make this game more difficult by describing the pictures with clues. For instance, instead of saying, "Bob's mother is giving him a birthday present," you could say: "In this picture Bob is very happy about something!"

Magic Hair Potion

Your child will love this activity. It is designed as an introduction to growing things. It should also provoke some "hairy" questions!

WHAT YOU NEED

One potato	Spoon
Moist cotton	Grass seed
Knife	Small dish of water

WHAT YOU AND YOUR CHILD DO

Cut off the very top of the potato and hollow out some of the pulp. Put damp cotton into the depression. Cut off the bottom of the potato to make a flat surface and stand it in a dish of shallow water. Sprinkle grass seed on the damp cotton. Water the seed lightly every day and keep water in the dish.

In about a week the potato should have a lovely crop of grassy hair. Decorate the potato with a nose, mouth, eyes, and ears.

Here are some questions to consider: How could the grass grow without dirt? What other things can we grow this way? What would happen if we used an apple? A grapefruit? How long do you think the "hair" will grow? What would happen if we put food coloring in the water?

45 Rhyme Time

Because rhyming is easy for most children, it creates "language confidence" at an early age. Here's a rhyming game to pull out of your hat anytime, anyplace!

Start by saying one word. The next player must say another word that rhymes with the previous word. When you have exhausted all possibilities, begin again with a new word.

46

Now You See It!

Look at part of an object and then guess what the whole object is. This simple activity cultivates inference skills.

Several large pictures from a magazine
Plain paper—make sure you can't see through it

Choose one of the pictures and cover it completely with the plain paper. Uncover a small area of the picture. See if your child can guess what it is. Keep uncovering the picture, little by little, until a correct guess is made. Now you take a turn. This isn't as easy as you think!

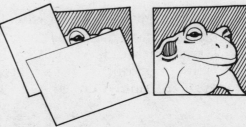

47 Newspaper Hunt

Although the price of the daily paper keeps climbing, it is still a great bargain as a teaching tool. The following activities reinforce inference and visual discrimination.

WHAT YOU NEED

Two copies of the same newspaper
Scissors

WHAT YOU AND YOUR CHILD DO

Cut out several pictures from your copy of the paper. Ask your child to find each of these pictures, one at a time, in the other copy of the paper.

Next cut out parts of some pictures and have your child use the segments to find the complete images. If your child is beginning to read, try this activity with words or headlines.

48 Building Blocks

A complete set of sturdy building blocks is one of the best educational investments you can make. Block construction builds visual and motor skills and provides rich opportunities for creative problem-solving. Blocks even introduce children to the basic laws of physics.

Make sure that your child reaps all the benefits of blocks play. It's easy. All you need to do is ask an occasional question. Here are some questions designed to develop a wide range of thinking skills, including classifying, defining spatial relationships, problem-solving, and predicting.

WHAT YOU NEED

A good set of building blocks

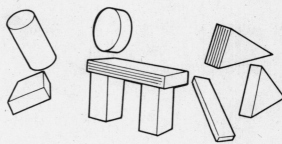

WHAT YOU AND YOUR CHILD DO

As you build with blocks, occasionally ask your child one of the following questions. Be certain that your question is appropriate, and don't bombard your engineer with all the questions at once.

"Look at this block. Can you find another one just like it?"

"What do you think would happen if we put this block here?"

"How many rectangles can you see?"

"When you put these two triangles together, what do they look like?"

"Can you find a block that is not big and not square?"

"What will happen if you put that big block on top?"

"Look, my hand is three blocks long. How many blocks long is your hand?"

"There are no doors. How will people get in?"

Hold up a small toy animal and a human figure. "Can you make a house for each of these? How will the houses look different?"

Decimal Duets

Here is a quick way to introduce your child to the world of decimals—and perhaps classical music, too.

A radio
Newspaper
radio schedule

Look over the radio schedule. Point out the call letter and numbers of a few stations. Read the descriptions of the kind of programs the stations present.

Have your child select a few stations and locate them on the radio. You can further enrich this simple activity by discussing what kind of music you hear—classical, rock, jazz?

Now, you tune in a station. See if your child can identify the type of music being played and identify the decimal call numbers of the station.

What Is a Rebus?

A *rebus* is puzzle made up of pictures that represent syllables or words. The rebus pictures are combined with letters and words to create a complete message. Here is a rebus:

 LOVE

Rebuses, which children love, are excellent stepping stones to reading. They stretch deductive thinking skills.

Paper
Pen   DON'T BOTHER ME!

Compose very simple rebus messages and place them where your child will spot them during the day—next to a toothbrush, a lunch box, pinned on a sweater, etc. Ask your child to decode the secret messages.

Here are some rebuses to get you going!

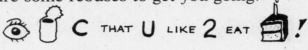 C THAT U LIKE 2 EAT !

 U GOODBYE.

Here are some more things your child can do with a rebus:

Write his name   Write a letter
Write his best friend's name   Write a short story

51 | Who's on First?

Sequencing, recall, ordinal numbers, auditory discrimination—you get it all in one easy game!

Show your child a sequence of two simple body movements. (Scratch your nose; clap your hands.) Ask your child to repeat the thing that you did *first*. Demonstrate another pair of simple movements. Ask your child to repeat the movement you made *second*.

Continue this game, progressing to a sequence of three or four movements. After each sequence, ask your child to repeat one specific movement.

This game is fun when the whole family plays, adding silly movements and sounds, the goofier, the better!

Flowering Onions

I hope this activity won't lead to tears. Whenever your plant experiments refuse to grow, take advantage of the opportunity for learning. Help your child figure out what might have gone wrong. Learning from mistakes is more than an old adage; it is the cornerstone of scientific discovery.

WHAT YOU NEED

One large onion
Three toothpicks
Glass of water

WHAT YOU AND YOUR CHILD DO

Place the onion in the top of the glass of water so that only the bottom of the onion is in the water. Stick the toothpicks into the onion to support it in the glass. Place the onion where it gets plenty of light.

Predict what will happen. Will it flower? Write down the prediction and, later, compare it with the actual results.

This experiment also works with potatoes.

53 Picture Starters

Crayons and creativity go hand in hand. Try this for a quick fix when your child is stuck inside and complaining of boredom.

WHAT YOU NEED

Crayons
Paper

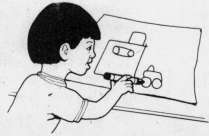

Suggest that your child draw a picture of one of the following:

What he or she will look like as an adult

What Mom or Dad looked like as a baby

A talking television

A machine that could clean his or her bedroom

A new kind of healthy food that would be more fun to eat than candy

A playground for animals

A restaurant for monsters

54 Remember the Dots

Here is an excellent way to practice memory, sequencing, and patterning skills.

A few pieces of opaque white paper

Colored paper, one sheet in each color: red, green, blue, yellow

One quarter

A pencil

Scissors

Trace the outline of the quarter ten times on each colored sheet of paper. Cut out the ten circles of each color. Give your child five of each color.

Place your dots in a simple pattern on a sheet of white paper. You don't have to use them all. Here's a simple pattern: one blue, two red, one green or one blue, two red, one green.

Tell your child to look at your dots and try to remember them. Cover your dots with another sheet of white paper. Ask your child to try to duplicate your pattern with his or her dots on a third sheet of white paper.

If this seems too difficult, make your patterns easier by using fewer dots.

55

Puppet Magic

Most young children can give a puppet show at the drop of a hat. It's important to provide opportunities to nurture this type of dramatic play, which is basic to the development of creative thinking. Making puppets is easy. You can use any combination of ice-cream sticks, paper bags, construction paper, socks, yarn, crayon, or markers.

I have always found, however, that children lose interest quickly unless they have a *stage*. A puppet without a stage is like a magician without a hat. A stage means a "real" show. You don't have to be a carpenter to make a stage. Here are two astonishingly simple ways to create a puppet stage.

Easy Puppet Theater

**WHAT
YOU
NEED**

Kitchen table
or card table

**WHAT
YOU
AND
YOUR
CHILD
DO**

Just turn over the table, crouch behind it, and perform!

Easy Puppet Theater

Kitchen table
or card table
Old sheet
Scissors

Cover the table with the sheet. Cut out a "window" in the middle of the sheet. Pin or tape scenery onto the sheet. Children can sit under the table and display their puppets through the hole.

56 | Feed the Birds

One of my children loves birds. The other loves peanut butter. With this activity I found a way to appeal to both and create a living science experiment.

One cup of peanut butter
Spatula or butter spreader
One large pine cone
String or cord

47

Spread the peanut butter all over the pine cone until it is covered. Although I recommend a spatula, my son likes to use his fingers for this part.

Attach the string to the pine cone. Hang it up. If no birds come in a few days, try hanging it in an area where you see birds often. Once the birds discover it, you can move it to a new place and they will follow.

There are many questions to think about while watching a feeder. Here are a few:

> Why do the birds like peanut butter?
>
> What else could you use that they would like?
>
> Why is it a good idea to use a pine cone? What else could you use?

Other suggestions:

> Get binoculars and take a closer look.
>
> Draw pictures of the birds. Do the same ones come back? How can you tell?

57 Puzzle Cups

When it comes to puzzles, I never met one I didn't like. They are all terrific for nurturing thinking skills. Even the simplest puzzle cultivates visual discrimination, inference skills, problem-solving skills, and small motor coordination. The only trouble with puzzles is their lack of "repeatability." Few children want to solve the same puzzle more than three or four times. This can get pretty expensive, so here's a way to make your own. My children like these because they are three-dimensional.

Twenty to thirty Styrofoam cups
Glue
Cardboard
Scissors

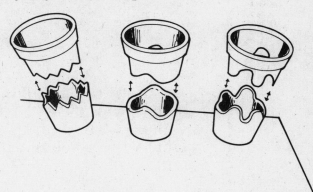

Cut each cup horizontally into two pieces, using jagged cuts so that the two pieces fit back together like jigsaw-puzzle pieces. Glue the bottom of each cup to a piece of cardboard, or put them all on one big piece.

Now mix up the tops and try to match the tops and bottoms. Use a timer for an extra challenge.

58 Plant Peekaboo

Plants need light. They even move around to find it. This is called *phototropism*, and even a very young child will be interested in this demonstration of it. This is a simple science activity that leaves a lasting impression.

One lima bean seed
Small pot
Potting soil
Small shovel or large spoon
Shoe box with lid
Scissors

Plant the seed in the pot. Make sure it gets plenty of light, and water it lightly every few days. Lima beans grow quickly and you should soon have a sprout.

When the sprout is about four inches high, put the plant into the shoe box. Cut a small, round hole in the box, at the same height as the top of the plant.

Close the box (except for the hole) and set it near a window, with the hole facing the window. After three or four days open the box. What has happened to the plant? Why do you think this happened?

59 Marvelous Memory

Memory skills are among the most important—and most overlooked—thinking skills. They are also among the most fun to practice.

A selection of familiar household objects, such as a glass, a bowl, a spoon, a comb, a brush, a pencil, a book

Take turns playing this classic memory game. Place four or five objects on a table and look at them very closely, one at a time, until you think you can remember them all. Now close your eyes as your partner removes one of the items and rearranges the rest. Which one is missing?

Here are several variations:

> Increase the number of objects on the table
>
> Remove more than one object
>
> Set a limit on the time given to study the objects
>
> Use items that are in the same category, but different in appearance, such as six different kinds of glasses, five books, a number of unpaired socks, etc.

60 Invisible Read-Alongs

Read-along books and tapes are among your best buys in educational toys. Here's a way to get even more educational value from them and a way to create your own. "Invisible" read-alongs promote listening and creative thinking skills.

WHAT YOU NEED

Pre-recorded story tapes
Tape player/recorder
A favorite book
A blank audio cassette
Microphone, if needed

WHAT YOU AND YOUR CHILD DO

Pick a read-along cassette and listen to it without looking at the book. A friend whose two girls share a room puts the tape player in the middle of the room each night as they lie in bed so they can listen to their favorite stories.

Select a favorite book for which there is *no* audio cassette. Invite your child to help you record the story on a blank tape. A very young child can participate by ringing a bell or tapping a glass with a spoon at the end of each page. Older children will enjoy reading parts of the story themselves and creating sound and music effects.

Don't be surprised to find yourself manufacturing an entire library of these homemade tapes. It's great fun when the whole family joins in. Then you have a treasured keepsake as well as a good story.

61 Secret Identity

Your child will enjoy this detective game which also polishes inference skills.

WHAT YOU NEED

Labels from empty boxes or cans of familiar household products
Scissors
Several plain envelopes or small plastic bags

WHAT YOU AND YOUR CHILD DO

Cut each label into several pieces. Put all the pieces of each label into an envelope or a small plastic bag. Be sure to keep each label in its own bag or envelope!

Remove one piece of a label. Which product is it? How many pieces does your child need to see before he or she can recognize the product?

62 | Number Words

Most of the number words defy phonetic decoding: they must be memorized on sight. Here is a way to give your child a head start on learning these words while practicing motor coordination.

WHAT YOU NEED

Chalk
Sidewalk
Rock or shoe heel*

WHAT YOU AND YOUR CHILD DO

Draw a hopscotch grid and label it by writing the number *words* in the boxes instead of the numerals. If your child has trouble identifying the words, write both the numeral and the word in each box. After a few games, erase the numerals.
Play hopscotch!

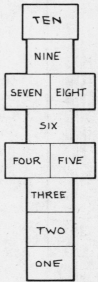

*Where I grew up we always used hopscotch "heels." We would ask a shoemaker for one, and it worked wonderfully. Elsewhere, children use rocks.

63 | Puzzles That Meet the Challenge

Bright children often find that simple jigsaw puzzles of up to fifteen pieces are too easy. On the other hand, sixty to one hundred pieces may be too much to handle.

With this simple idea you can enhance your child's small motor skills as well as the critical thinking skills of inference and sequencing.

WHAT YOU NEED

Large piece of cardboard or poster board
Marker
One fifty- to one hundred-piece puzzle
Glue

WHAT YOU AND YOUR CHILD DO

Complete the puzzle together, placing the pieces on the cardboard. Glue the outside border pieces to the board to make a frame. As you remove each remaining piece, outline its proper position on the cardboard. Your child should now be able to do a tough puzzle independently or with a minimum of help.

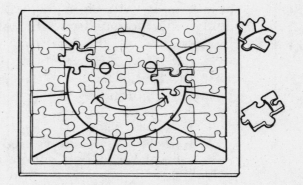

64 | The Golden Door

For some the neighborhood library is a golden door to a magical land which they enter again and again. For others a library is the place they go only when they have to. Your example and attitude will set the tone for your child. Here are some ways to open the golden door.

A library card
Calendar
Marker or pencil

Make trips to the library a family outing. Try to go every other week, but no less than once a month! A brilliant woman whose two children are both enthusiastic readers told me that she was raised in a family of readers. "Every week," she says, "my mother, father, sisters, and I would walk to the library and fill a shopping cart with books." Her reading habits and those of her children attest to the enduring power of youthful impressions.

Have a special container in which you keep all library books. It can be a cardboard box, a basket, a plastic crate, even a plastic trash can. This eliminates the frantic searching for books on library day.

As soon as you get home from the library, have your child help you mark the calendar with the due date of the books and the *number* of books to be returned that day.

Most parents select books from the fiction section. Don't forget the nonfiction! There are wonderful picture books on everything: bugs, robots, animals, dolls, dinosaurs, blood, flowers, etc. Let the librarian guide you to the nonfiction picture books and easy-readers that suit your child's interests. As you browse through the library you will also find many children's books shelved in places other than the children's section.

As soon as possible, have your child get a library card, and help him or her keep a personal calendar recording the due date and number of books borrowed.

Most libraries have several different versions of the most famous fairy tales and folk tales. Have the librarian help you find two or three versions of the same story. Encourage your child to compare them. Point out the illustrations. How do they look different? The same? Some stories even have different endings. Why? Which one do you like best?

If you make the library part of your life, your child will follow suit. For instance, when we needed to buy a new dishwasher, we went to the library to look up the consumer ratings of various brands. If you are planning a family vacation, check out books on the area you will be visiting. Even adults are surprised when they find how many services libraries offer.

65

Simple Scale

This activity grew out of a center in my classroom. My own children loved it, too. It is another excellent vehicle for fostering skills of estimation, prediction, and inference.

**WHAT
YOU
NEED**

Wire hanger
Two empty soft margarine or sour cream containers—the same size
String
Scissors
Two chairs
Broom
Small objects (keys, crayons, blocks, pencils, etc.)

Cut three holes, evenly spaced apart, beneath the rim of each container. Use string to tie the containers to each end of the hanger. Try to use equal amounts of string to get the containers to hang as evenly as possible.

Balance a broom between two chairs. Hang the hanger on the end of the broom. Select pairs of objects and predict which will be the heaviest. Test your hypotheses by using the scale.

For more of a challenge, predict which item out of three or four is the heaviest. How can you use this scale to test the answers?

66 | Points of View

You can help your child develop the ability to consider issues and events from many points of view. This ability cannot be underestimated. It not only sets the stage for creative thinking; it provides practice in looking at all sides of a situation, an important component of decision-making. Seeing through other eyes also generates empathy and compassion—important things for important thinkers.

Paper
Pencil
Crayons or markers

Make a picture of something from an animal's point of view. Pretend to be a dog, a cat, an ant, a bird, or any other animal. How would a worm see the garden? How would a bird see the backyard? How does a cat see the living room?

If your child balks at drawing, try this activity without pencil or paper. Ask your child to describe how a bug would see your front door or what a fish would say as it looks out of its bowl.

67 Shell Game

This classic game is terrific for improving skills of concentration, observation, and memory.

Four cups or glasses—make sure you can't see through them
One small ball or other object that fits under the cups

Place the ball under one of the cups. Move the cups around. Where is the ball now? Take turns mixing the cups and guessing. My sons love to do this—with a great deal of theatrical "Abracadabra" hoopla.

You can use grapes, raisins, or blueberries and eat the right answers!

68 | Balancing Act

This is another quick way to develop concentration and coordination.

Chalk
Cup of water
Egg
Spoon

Find a flat, safe outdoor area and draw a circular track. Walk on the circle without stepping off of it, placing one foot in front of the other. Next, walk the circle while carrying a cup of water, trying not to spill any.

Can you walk the circle while balancing an egg on a spoon? On rainy days, I hard-boil the eggs and use the kitchen floor. For variety, you can draw different shapes and use different items.

69 | Watermelon Time

The skill of estimation is getting a lot of formal attention in the schools. Estimating is more than a lucky guess. It is a reasonable guess made after sizing up all available clues. This summertime activity can cultivate estimating skills, while entertaining an entire family for at least one picnic!

One ripe watermelon
A knife
Lots of napkins
A ruler or any other measuring tool

Estimate how many seeds are in the watermelon. You may cut a slice or use a ruler to help with your guesses. Solicit estimates from everyone in the family and write down the estimates. How did each person make his estimate?

Find out how many seeds are in the watermelon. This is the best part! Whose estimate was closest?

70 Mirror Image

This game is often used in theater improvisation classes. It requires supreme concentration.

Sit or stand directly across from each other. When you move, your child must try to follow your movements as closely as possible. Then you must follow his or her movements.
You must think hard
in order to follow,
rather than anticipate,
your partner's moves.

71 Snow Painting

Turn any day into a "snowy," creative day—and get the inside of your windows clean at the same time! You must supervise this activity closely.

Windows
Shaving cream

Give your child a small bowl of shaving cream and tell him or her that he or she can use it to finger-paint on the inside of a window. When done, let the cream dry. Then wipe the window with a cloth. You will be amazed at how clean your window will be!

Experimenting with different materials and textures encourages a child to think creatively and to discover physical properties. If you are squeamish about shaving cream on the windows, move the above activity to the bathtub. I know another parent who lets her child finger-paint in the tub with chocolate pudding, yogurt, and whipped cream.

72 Scavenger Hunt

This instant idea is full of fun and reinforces an understanding of attributes, categorizing, and a variety of basic academic skills.

Household items
Bags or pillowcases

Go on a scavenger hunt. Pick a category and find items that fit into it. Here are some suggestions:

Shapes—find three things shaped like circles, three like squares, three like triangles, etc.

Consonants—find as many things as you can that start or end with a given letter

Pairs—find things that come in pairs

Colors

Soft things

Old things

Things made of paper

Things made of metal

It's a good idea to have a time limit, and be sure to supervise children out-of-doors.

73 Touch Me

Here's an activity designed to help expand your child's vocabulary and ability to make tactile discriminations.

A park or backyard

One shopping bag

Four to eight small sandwich-size plastic bags

Index cards

Markers

Write a texture word on each index card. Here are some: soft, hard, smooth, bumpy, prickly, squishy, sharp, sticky. Read them aloud and review the meaning of each one. Place each card in a plastic bag.

Accompany your child on the search as he or she places items in the correct bag. Individual bags can be carried inside a bigger shopping bag.

Are there items that fit *two* words? Is a worm soft and squishy? Is something sharp and prickly? Can your child find something smooth, sharp, and soft? Can you figure out how to bag or label an object that belongs in more than one category? (Bring along extra bags and a marker.)

74 | Museum Musings

What do you remember most about your last museum outing with a young child? Aching feet? Paying eight dollars for a hamburger? Here are some tips for making your next museum trek everything you hoped it would be.

A good day for
a museum outing

Plan your visit for one hour—not one minute more. Most parents make the mistake of making a museum outing an entire day or morning proposition. Your child won't enjoy three hours in a museum any more than you will. Sometimes museums are far away, and it does seem a shame to leave so soon after you get there. But in the long run, it will be worth it! Your child will have a memory of a pleasant time and be anxious to return.

Visit the gift shop *first*. Pick out two or three post-cards of things you want to see "in person." After your one-hour visit, pick out two more postcards with items to see next time. Then make another definite date, even if it is six months away. Tape the postcards on or near a calendar to mark the day.

When looking at a painting, encourage thought by asking an occasional question:

"Where would you draw another person in this painting?"

"Look at the picture closely. Now close your eyes and tell me three things you saw."

"The title of this is '_____.' What would *you* call it?"

75 | Weigh To Go

Children love to get on the scale. Always seize such an opportunity for making the most of a natural inclination.

Bathroom scale

Assorted household objects heavy enough to register on a bathroom scale

Assemble three to five objects of similar size and different weights. Make sure the objects are quite different in weight. If they are too close, the difference may not show up on this type of scale.

Ask your child to predict which will be the heaviest and which the lightest, and put the objects in order from the lightest to the heaviest. Now test the hypothesis by weighing the objects.

76 | Party Time

When company is coming, it's a good idea to get some help and at the same time reinforce positional concepts.

Index cards
Markers
Pencil
Paper

Write a guest's name on each index card. Read each name card. Decorate each card.

Put one card in its proper place on the table and then give your child simple directions for placing the rest. Here are some examples of ways to give directions that are clear, but also thought-provoking:

"Put Mike's card next to Morgan's."

"Nina will sit between Jon and Mike."

"Nora is to the left of Mike."

The Wishing Box

This is adapted from a classroom reading center. It was always a favorite with me and my students.

Old mail-order toy catalogs
Scissors
Paste
Index cards
Markers
Shoe box or container of similar size

Cut out pictures of anything your child would like to have. Paste each picture on an index card. These are the "wish" cards. Put them in the box.

On blank index cards, write the word or words that describe each picture card. Put these "name" cards in a separate pile. Older children can cut out the printed catalog descriptions and paste those to the name cards.

When you have filled the box with enough wish cards, you can play a simple game. Mix up the wish cards. Each player closes his or her eyes and picks out three wish cards. Match the wish cards with the name cards.

How Long Is It?

Even very young children feel successful as they attempt to match straws while building visual discrimination and inference skills.

WHAT YOU NEED

Thirty straws
Scissors
White drawing paper
Marker
Ruler

WHAT YOU AND YOUR CHILD DO

Cut the straws into four different lengths: tiny, short, medium, and long. Draw each of these four lines on the paper. Review the sizes with your child.

Pile up the straws. Select one, hold it up, and say whether it is tiny, short, medium, or long. Place the straw on the paper to see if you are correct. If so, keep the straw. If not, put it back. The person with the most straws wins. When my children get them all correct, they get a large, cool glass of milk or juice.

79 | Conservation

Conservation: objects can change their shape, but remain quantitatively the same, as long as nothing has been added or removed. Eight ounces of milk looks different in a wide glass than in a tall, thin glass. Most children under the age of seven, however, will say that the taller glass has more milk.

Many child-development experts assert that a child cannot learn this concept until seven or older. But younger children should nevertheless be given the opportunity to experiment and learn by discovery. Here are a few ways to encourage this independent research.

Three glasses: two the same size and one taller and narrower

Milk, juice, or colored water

Two balls of clay or Play Doh

Fill the two same size glasses half full of liquid. Ask our child if there is the same amount in each glass. Now pour the liquid from one glass into the tall, thin glass. Ask: "Is there more, less, or the same amount in the tall glass?"

Try this every few months and see if your child eventually begins to see that the amounts are the same. It's especially helpful if you allow your child to pour the liquid back and forth on his or her own.

Here's another method for discovering the same concept: take two balls of Play Doh that are the same size. Flatten one out. Ask: "Are the balls still the same size?"

Keep in mind that it is not as important to teach this concept as it is to enjoy experimenting.

80 Goofy Nursery Rhymes

This activity is great for enhancing oral language skills and creative thinking. It's also lots of fun.

A book of nursery rhymes

HICKORY, DICKORY, DOCK,
WHERE IS MY BRAND NEW CLOCK?
THE CLOCK STRUCK TWO
IT'S IN MY SHOE,
AND NOW IT'S HARD
TO WALK!

Read or recite a favorite nursery rhyme. Then make up a new, silly verse for the rhyme. Here's an example:

At three years of age my children couldn't do this, nor did they think it was funny. But at five and a half they thought it was a scream. They especially like to include "disgusting" and "gross" details.

If your child isn't ready for this yet, try it again in six months to a year!

81 Simple Sundial

On a sunny day enjoy a science-math-history lesson all rolled into fun.

Twelve ice-cream sticks
One wooden dowel
A sunny day

Briefly explain that long ago people did not have clocks. Ask your child to think of ways that people might tell time without a clock. Your child may come up with this answer, or you may eventually supply it: "People used the sun to tell time. They made a sundial. Now we can make one."

Find an area outside that gets sunlight all day long. Push a dowel into this sunny spot. On the hour, mark the location of the dowel's shadow with an ice-cream stick. Write the hour on the stick and insert it into the ground. Do this every hour. Ask your child how it will be possible to mark all the hours.

Leave the clock in place and check it for accuracy in a few days and then weeks, if possible. Is it still correct? Why or why not?

82 | Spin Me a Yarn

This is another classroom idea that has become a family tradition. A simple prop diminishes stage fright, even in grownups. It is much easier to tell a story when you know you aren't responsible for the whole thing.

Pieces of string, yarn, ribbon, cord, rope, etc.

Tie pieces of string, yarn, etc. together at uneven intervals. Make the knots at least twelve inches apart, with some as far apart as a yard. Roll the pieces into a ball.

Begin the story. As you speak, slowly unroll the string. When you get to a knot, stop and give the ball to the next person. Now it's his or her turn to continue the story and keep talking and unwinding—until a knot comes up. Continue until the ball is completely unwound.

Memories Are Made of This

Many people attribute good memory skills to luck. "He was just born with a good memory!" Heredity plays some role, but memory skills can be learned and improved. It is important to cultivate memory skills, since they play a key role in virtually all other learning.

WHAT YOU NEED

Six pairs of identical words, letters, or pictures cut to fit inside the pockets of an egg carton

One egg carton

Scissors

Paste or glue

WHAT YOU AND YOUR CHILD DO

Cut the egg carton in half, making sure to leave the top attached to the bottom. Glue six pictures, words, or letters to the top of the carton on the outside. Put the other six pictures inside the egg pockets, in a different order. Close the carton.

Look at the pictures on the top until you think you can remember each one. (Later you may want to try this with a time limit). Open the carton and rearrange the pictures in the order that you saw on the top.

For older children, try this with twelve pairs of pictures and a whole egg carton.

84 Rice Forecast

Here's another activity to practice estimating, predicting, and testing hypotheses. Children find the funnel and scoop irresistible.

Ten glass jars of varying sizes
Masking tape
Two to six pounds of rice
Funnel
Scoop

WHAT YOU AND YOUR CHILD DO

Use the tape to mark off different "fill" levels on each jar. It's a good idea to let your child practice using the funnel and scoop to fill a jar.

Look at the first jar and estimate how many scoops of rice it will take to fill it to the line. Write down this prediction. Test the prediction by actually filling the jar. How many scoops did it take? Write down the results.

Which jar will take the most scoops? The least? Will any be the same? Don't forget to record all predictions and results. In this way you set an important example in scientific accuracy.

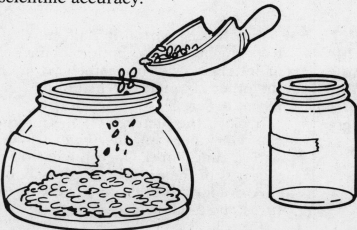

85 Walking, Yes Indeed!

A walk through the neighborhood or around the block is relaxing and fun. It is a natural exercise in critical and creative thinking. You and your child will find yourselves observing, wondering, and dreaming as you go. Here are some suggestions for getting more thoughts per footstep.

WHAT YOU NEED

Comfortable shoes or boots
Paper
Pencil
Crayons or markers

WHAT YOU AND YOUR CHILD DO

Before you go out, decide on your route. From your memory of that route make a list of answers to these or similar questions:

How many houses or buildings will we pass?
How many stories in each building?
What color are the buildings?
Are there signs or parking meters? How many?
Are there stores, schools, parks? How many?

Record your answers and your child's separately.
Now take the walk and check your answers! Who got the most answers correct?

It's in the Bag

Here's another activity designed to enhance classification skills. It also makes an excellent travel game.

WHAT YOU NEED

Thirty index cards
Two paper bags

WHAT YOU AND YOUR CHILD DO

Take five index cards and write the name of a different category on each. Some examples are: sports, cars, boys' names, girls' names, games, animals, foods, cities, countries. Put the cards in one of the paper bags.

Write one letter of the alphabet on each of the remaining cards, omitting only the letter X. Place these cards in the other paper bag.

Shake the bags. Pick one card from each bag. You will then have one letter card and one category card. Name something in that category that begins with the letter on the other card. If you are right, keep the letter card, draw another, and try again. If you are wrong, put both cards back and give the next player a turn.

The person with the most letter cards wins!

Listening Mystery

This activity forces a child to listen and concentrate. You can put it together in a few minutes with just about anything you have on hand.

WHAT YOU NEED

Six to twelve lunch-size paper bags

Assorted household items that will shake inside the bags: rice, sugar, beans, sand, pebbles, paper clips, crayons, spoons, dry cereal, etc.

WHAT YOU AND YOUR CHILD DO

Divide each item into two equal portions, and put each portion in a different bag. Fold down the tops of the bags so that the contents cannot be seen. Mix up the bags.

Pick up one bag and shake it. Put the bag aside. Now try to find the other bag containing the same item.

This game is more difficult than it seems. You might want to start with only three or four pairs of bags. Make sure that you divide the items as equally as possible.

88 Blushing Celery

This is a classic science experiment that used to be taught in the third or fourth grade. Recently I saw a teacher demonstrate it to a preschool class. They not only loved it; they were able to explain what it meant. You will have to wait at least an hour to see results.

Red or blue food coloring
Stalk of celery with leaves on top
Glass of water
Knife or scissors

Explain that plants have tiny tubes inside that carry food and water from the roots up to the leaves and flowers.

Mix the food coloring into the water. Cut off the bottom of the celery. Explain that you are going to do an experiment that will show how these tubes work.

Place the celery in the colored water. Be sure that the leaves are on top! Wait an hour and see what happens. As more time goes by, the effect will be very marked. Come back the next day for some stunning red celery!

If possible, try this same experiment with a white carnation or daisy.

89 Name Game

This is a variation of a pencil-and-paper word game that is a favorite of older children. Younger children can often read their name and the names of relatives and friends before they can read other words. If your child can read names, this game will help cultivate sight reading and visual discrimination skills.

Pencil and paper

First make a list of names that your child can read. Keep it simple. Three or four names is fine. Here's an example:

Name List

Mike
Jonathan
Erik
Susan

```
J O N A T H A N X
M A Z Q X R T M S
S U S A N X B I T
W E S T M R S K U
Q W E R I K M E O
```

Review the list and make sure your child can read each name. Now make a "word search" puzzle and conceal the names in the puzzle. The names can go across or up and down. Use capital letters.

Have your child circle the names. As your child's skills increase, you can increase the name list, or do a puzzle without a name list.

90 Treasure Hunt

This game is truly a treasure trove of reasoning skills that stretch deductive thinking ability.

Old magazines or newspapers
Index cards
Scissors
Wrapping paper
Ribbon
Glue

77

Plan a treasure hunt using picture clues. For instance, cut out a picture of a sofa. If this is Clue #1, your child will look under the sofa for the next clue. There he or she will find the picture that leads to the next spot.

Make the hunt as long or as short as you'd like. The treasure can be anything—a box of raisins, a new book, a small toy. Wrap it up with ribbon and paper to enhance its value.

91 Alphabet Ball Bounce

"A, my name is Alice and I come from Alabama, where I sell apples." Familiar? I remember spending much of an entire summer bouncing a ball on the front porch and going through the alphabet over and over. You probably did, too. But you may be amazed, as I was, at how few children play this simple game today. Don't let your child miss it! This classic game is excellent for teaching language skills and cultivating coordination.

A ball with a lot of bounce

Take turns bouncing the ball. Fill in the blanks for each letter: *(letter)*, my name is _____, and I come from _____, where I sell _____.

When you cannot complete the line, or if you miss a bounce, the ball passes to the next player. Older children may smirk and say this is "baby stuff," but pretty soon they will join in!

Supermarket Science

Children are never too young to begin developing skills of scientific inquiry. You don't have to be a scientist yourself to nurture this skill. But you need to know an important trick: how to get your child to *ask questions*. Pose questions that lend themselves to experimentation and discovery. For example, if your child comments that the squirrels seem to prefer the peanut butter sandwich he or she left outside to acorns, suggest that you find a way to see if this is really true. Stay alert, and you will find many ways to elicit hands-on experiments. Here are a few ideas to use as you shop in the supermarket.

WHAT YOU AND YOUR CHILD DO

While shopping with your child, ask one or more of the following questions. You don't have to know the answers, but you do have to be willing to help check things out. For example, why not put some oranges in the freezer and see what happens?

What did we buy today that grew on a tree?

Why do certain things have to be kept cold?

Why don't we have to keep cereal in the refrigerator? What would happen to it if we did?

Why don't we find apples or oranges in the freezer?

Do you know where this food comes from? Can we find it on the map when we get home? How do you think the food got here? Was it important for the food to travel quickly?

What happens to a banana when you drop it? (Try this at home, of course!)

Here are an apple and an orange, both the same size. Do you think one will weigh more? Which?

Once you get the hang of this, you will find lots of opportunities to encourage a scientific approach. If your child is helping you bake bread, be willing to see what happens if you put in less yeast, more yeast, let it rise longer, or not long enough. You must be willing to experiment, and also willing to look up information. In this way, you not only show your child that science is a natural, sometimes funny, and exciting subject, but you will probably learn quite a bit yourself!

93 Odd Man Out

It doesn't seem too tough to figure out that a fork, knife, and spoon are similar because they are all eating implements. But the child who masters the skill of noting similarities may one day investigate common microbes or write a book on the similarities and differences of Eastern and Western cultures. Remember, thinking skills are important because they can be applied to anything!

WHAT YOU NEED

Simple household items
Tray or shoe box

80

Find three items that are related in some way (eating utensils, kinds of food, things that start with the same letter, toys, tools, etc.). Place the three items on the tray. Add one more item that does *not* belong with this group. Mix up the items. Have your child select the item that does not belong.

You can make this more difficult if the fourth item is *related* to the others, but still not the same. This way, your child has to look for more subtle relationships. Here are some examples:

knife, teaspoon, fork, *napkin*

apple, banana, pear, *potato*

cake, cookie, doughnut, *bread*

coffee cup, mug, drinking glass, *mixing bowl*

pen, pencil, marker, *eraser*

94 | Coconut Challenge

When I taught first grade, my classroom was next to a rather quiet kindergarten class. One day it was so noisy next door that I peeked in to check, assuming that the teacher was away. She wasn't. The class was involved in the "Coconut Challenge." I have used this activity at home and in the classroom again and again. It is a natural, wonderful way to sharpen problem-solving skills.

One unopened coconut

Look at a coconut. Talk about what it is and what is inside of it. Hold it, shake it, rub it, tap it, etc.

Here's the challenge: "You can taste this coconut *if you* can figure out how to open it."

With your close supervision, allow your child to try any reasonable idea. Provide safe tools. This challenge may take days, hours, or merely minutes. You can usually find the solution in a good cookbook—if you need it.

95 Egg Carton Patterns

You can make this activity difficult or easy, but either way it is an effective game to reinforce sequencing and inference skills.

Empty egg carton
Objects small enough to fit inside the carton (coins, marbles, cotton balls, paper clips, etc.)

Use the small objects to make a pattern inside the carton. For example, place two coins, one marble, two paper clips, and one cotton ball in the top row of the carton.

Repeat the pattern in the bottom row, but leave out the last item. Have your child put in that one.

96 Math Munchies

Math drill can be tedious, but even the most theoretical of mathematicians must know the basic facts. You can use this activity for drill.

Small edible items: pretzel sticks, grapes, popcorn, carrot sticks, raisins

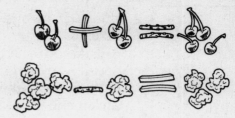

Use the edible items to show math problems. You can cross carrot or pretzel sticks to make plus signs. Two parallel pretzel sticks are good equal signs. Form the answer with the goodies. Correct answers can be eaten!

97 A Steady Clip

Children love to weigh and measure. Here is a family activity that develops skills of prediction, estimation, and problem-solving. Like conservation, concepts of precise measurement are not easily mastered. Allow your child a chance to experience, experiment, and discover.

A large box of paper clips, all clips the same size
Felt-tipped pen
Large piece of paper or tagboard

Choose an object, such as a large book or a small tabletop. Measure this object with your child's hand. How many hands long is it?

Now measure that same object with *your* hand. How many hands long is it? Discuss why there is a difference in the measurements. Explain why people need to measure things using some tool that is always the same size.

Take out the paper clips. Ask your child to check and see if they are the same size. Repeat your measuring experiment, measuring by lining up the paper clips along the edge of the object. Now do it again. Do you get the same measurement?

You can clip the paper clips together to make a measuring stirp and measure other objects. Guess how many paper clips long different objects will be. Write down the guesses and the actual answers.

In my classroom we added a creative writing lesson. As we were discussing what would happen if people measured things with their hands and feet, the children began laughing uproariously as they listed the absurd possibilities of such a measuring system. We ended up writing a class story about "The Nosy Kingdom," a place where people use their noses to measure. Your child might like writing, dictating, or telling you such a story!

98 Around the World

Invest in some inexpensive maps and put them up where the whole family can refer to them often. Make maps part of your routine. It's easy to find a world map and a U.S. map. Try to get a city and state map, too. Your local chamber of commerce may have them. Here are some tips for awakening an interest in geography.

WHAT YOU NEED

Maps
Thumbtacks or pins
String

Photos of distant family members and friends
Old letters or postcards

Children love to see where relatives and friends live. You can paste or tack small pictures directly onto the maps near the correct cities or towns. You can tape the pictures on the periphery of the map and use string to mark a line from the photo to the city. Mark the points of origin of letters or postcards on the map in the same way.

Look at the labels of your favorite food products or toys. Locate the city in which they are made. If possible, cut off a label and post it on the map. Ask your child how this product got from its point of origin to the place where you bought it.

If you are planning a business trip or a vacation, plot your route on the map. American families move often. Make the most of it! Mark the map with pictures of your old house or neighborhood. A child can plot his or her "life story" on the map. "Here's a picture of me when I was a baby in Baltimore. Here I am when I was two years old in Los Angeles."

Laminated maps are a real plus. You can mark them with a grease pencil and then wipe them clean with a tissue.

99 Concentration

There are many commercially available memory games, but a deck of cards will do the trick easily.

One deck of cards

Use only the red or the black cards. Remove the face cards. Place the cards face down, in rows, on the table. Uncover one card and then another, trying to make a match. When correct, the player keeps the cards and takes another turn. If there is no match, the next player takes a turn. As players gain expertise, add more cards.

100 Guess-timate

Here's another chance to practice estimating and inference skills.

A jar
Enough of one thing to fill the jar (paper clips, coins, beans, marbles)

Guess how many objects you can pull out of the jar in one handful. Write down the guess. Remove one handful of objects and count them. Record the results. How close was your guess?

Have your child do the same thing.

Now that you know how many objects make up one handful, you can try to figure out how many objects there are in the jar. Guess how many handfuls of things it took to fill the jar, and then calculate the total number of objects. You will have to do the multiplication for your child—but let him or her make his or her own guess. Ask other members of the family to guess, and record all the guesses.

Finally, carefully count the objects. Your child can help with this.

Who made the best guess? Ask that person how he or she figured it out.

Flat and Fancy Fruit

I never have trouble getting children into the kitchen for "cooking chemistry." Here is a recipe for a fruit roll that is healthier than most commercially available ones. It is sloooow-cooking and will tie up your oven for a long time, but it is an excellent demonstration of evaporation.

WHAT YOU NEED

Enough of one of the following fruits to make one cup of puree: bananas, apples, apricots, peaches, prunes, pineapples, nectarines, strawberries, or blueberries

One teaspoon of honey

Oil

Small cookie sheet

Blender

Plastic wrap

WHAT YOU AND YOUR CHILD DO

Preheat the oven to 200 degrees. Put the fruit in the blender. Blend well, until you have a cupful. Add honey and blend well. Lightly grease the pan. Pour the fruit-and-honey mix into the pan. It should be about ¼ inch deep.

Bake for four to six hours, turning the cookie sheet every hour or so. When the fruit is congealed, it is done. While still warm, carefully peel it off the cookie sheet. Put it on a sheet of plastic wrap. Let the fruit sheet cool.

Once it is cool, you can roll up the fruit in the plastic wrap. If your child doesn't eat it all, you can keep it wrapped in plastic and store it in a jar. What happened to the fruit? How did this happen? Why?

Answers

Solution to Egg Drop

What You Need

Bucket
Water
Plastic wrap
Raw egg

What You and Your Child Do

Fill a bucket about ¾ full of water. Drape a piece of plastic wrap over the top. Be sure that equal amounts of the wrap hang over each side. Spread out the plastic, but *don't* pull it tight. Allow some slack. Drop your egg! It should not break, as it is now cushioned by the air *and* the water.